Through My Eyes

Eleanor Barlow

BookLeaf Publishing

India | USA | UK

Presentation by *BookLeaf Publishing*

Web: www.bookleafpub.com

E-mail: info@bookleafpub.com

ISBN: 9789363301184

First edition 2024

To all the NHS staff who work so tirelessly. A big thank you for all that you do.

ACKNOWLEDGEMENT

To my friends and family that have encouraged and supported me.

To all the nurses, mental health workers and doctors in all the hospitals I have stayed in; a big thank you for the help and support you gave me. I also want to give a special thank you to all the staff at Primrose Ward in Arbury Court for their outstanding care of me over the many months that I was a patient there.

And lastly I want to say a massive thank you to Helen my psychologist. Who I feel truly blessed to have been working with this year. She has helped me to have a better understanding of my thoughts and feelings, my inner strengths and the way I view myself. Helen truly is amazing and I can't thank her enough.

PREFACE

This poetry book celebrates how I see the people that have come into my life and how much they have contributed into making my life better. It has been a rough couple of years and this poetry book explores not only the turbulence but also the progress I have made and the people who have helped me along the way.

Dear Dad,

I sometimes feel like I am cracking inside
And I haven't been the same since you died

There is so much I didn't know about you
That I wish you had stayed and pulled through

As I have so much I want to say
That I wish we had one more day

Because there is a lot I wanted to ask
But you hid behind your brave mask

I nearly joined you last year
As I was flying so high through the atmosphere

I don't want to end the same way
But I struggle to have reasons to stay

Especially with the sadness that I feel
Which is often too much for me to deal

I carry a piece of your pain
And I understand now how it drove you insane

I know you have been dead a while

But I really do miss your voice and smile

I really wish I could see you once more
To run to you as you come through the front
door

Because I am starting to forget your face
Even though I know you are watching from a
heavenly place

I really do miss you
And so do all the family too

Please know I am not mad
I am just sad

Because you carried around this crater like hole
That eventually engulfed your beautiful soul

Which had soldiered on for so long
Burdening the pain from the past in the form of
a song

Yet you had made the decision and it was your
choice
I just wish I'd been there to be a reasoning voice

But you found yourself alone at the end
Except for the tree who was your friend

I am not going to say goodbye
As I will be with you when I die

The Ticking Clock

Living for the moment
That has been an gone

Time seems suspended
As tomorrow may never come

Life is so fleeting
As time trickles by

Because no one lives forever
As we all shall one day die

Overdose

5

Lying in the hospital bed
Barely alive but not dead

Machines were beeping
In a coma I was sleeping

My body was healing
My mind was unfeeling

Spiralling Down

I want to die
And please don't ask why
I just do
And its not because of you
It will be tough
But you did your best
To pull me through
But you couldn't save me
As my mind and body wanted to be free
I just can't see all that you see
And I'm not sorry
I am choosing my path
My road
And my end
I had to fall
And fall I did
Well more like slid
Into a coma like sleep
That was so deep
This is me making the final leap
But the memories we share are yours to keep
And please don't weep
As I'm in a better place
Heaven I think?
So far out in space

I'm at peace
Now with the stars
Looking down on you
And oh I'm so proud
So proud of everyone of you
I hope you can feel that too
I really did love all of you
Please know that
In your hearts
And in your soul
Mine was just too sad
Too dark like coal
I had to say goodbye
As I was so tired of being 'Miss Happy'
When in fact I was feeling rather crappy
And this is not me lying
It was my soul which was crying
To end my pain
Which drove me insane
And I was so tired of driving in the fast lane
I now feel light like a dove
Soaring high above
As it's now my time
I feel free
And I am now ready
My spirit is steady
To leave this beautiful world
And take my place
In the heavens

To act as an angel
For you
Watching over you
Day and night
Oh you are such a precious sight
And I am still with you
In spirit
Looking
Laughing
And loving you
From afar
I am that twinkling star
So please don't cry
As you will be with me when you die
Where we will be able to roam the sky
Love you
Forever
And
Always

Farewell 2021

9

Mixing
Sipping
Tripping
My mood is slowly dipping

The world is falling all around
And I am slowly sinking into the solid ground

I am so tired of the daily grind
And I am slowly beginning to lose my mind
As the voices have begun to shout
And I am slowly starting to tap out

I have abdicated my god-given crown
As I am just a fraud and a decrepit clown

I am so lost internally in a chaotic place
While the world carries on slowly turning in
space

I can no longer see
And my spirit just wants to be set free
Because its struggling with this life
And cannot cope with all the strife

Is there fun to be had?!
As I cannot find it which is making me sad

My mental health is holding on by a strand
And this year I probably have spent well over 12
grand
Whilst being so high up in the atmosphere
For the better part of the year

And I am struggling to cope with all the
challenges sent my way
And it's difficult to listen to what people have to
say

Like why is life so Goddamn hard
This is not me wanting your pity or a sympathy
card!
It is just me being honest on how I feel
As I struggle to know what is right or real

I find it challenging to look after my health
Especially when I do not like or care about
myself

I have a poor diet
And my body is now taking a stand and starting
to riot
As it really does need some recovery time
To heal before embarking on the upward climb

I now feel a lightness as I breathe the heavenly
air
And life is more manageable because I can feel
the love of the people that care

I feel blessed to have come out the other side
As 2021 has been one hell of a journey and a
bumpy ride

I am so thankful to have made it through
And I want to thank all the doctors and nurses
for all that they do
And thank my family and friends for sticking by
me too

Time With You

You give me space to breathe,
and reflect
To pause
And take a minute
To just be

We take stock
Of the past
The present
And the future

Taking time to
Invest
Work
And apply

Trusting
The process
And sharing
The load

Being open
And honest
And staying true
With ourselves

Developing boundaries
And asking for help
Remembering to check in
And to check out

Learning
To move forward
And beyond
Our own limits

By working harmoniously
With the intricacies
Of the memories
We call life

Yet time stops
For a moment
When I'm talking, laughing,
and smiling with you

That it almost feels like a dream
A fairy tale
Or like a shooting star
In the night sky

There is light and healing
That you bring
A warmth

Which touches my skin

That I feel safe
At peace
And blessed
To have you

The Universe Within My Mind

There was something inside
That I couldn't quite fathom
But I knew it was something
That needed exploring

I was starting to question
If I wanted answers
But how would they help
My confused state of mind

Which was spinning in circles
Around the same spot
To a tune lost in time
That had long been forgot

Time standing still
But my mind racing on
Alone in my universe
That was now home

The waves of emotion
Were crashing around
In this new founded world
Without heaven or hell

Yet the merry-go-round
That once was called life
Was the start and end
Of the time itself

Angel Angie

Oh my dearest Angie,
My favourite blue minion
What would I do without you?
I would be so lost
So melancholy

It makes me bereft when I don't get to see you
My little heart breaks
And when you are around the floor shakes
As you are a whirlwind of fire
Never ceasing to tire

Oh Angie my love
Words fail me on how wonderful you are
You truly are a shining star
Burning the candle at both ends
That I'm sure we will be bosom friends

Love you more than you could know
Or what I could express or show
From your little Clark shoes
To your curly Afro mop
And let's not forget your halo that rests on top
You are smart, sexy and have more moves than
J-Lo!

As whenever I see you, you are always on the go

You have been there for me through thick and
thin
Especially when my head and heart would start
to spin
And you were always there to help quiet the din

You were there with me in 2021
And that admission was far from fun
It was comforting seeing you again in 2022
And oh how I have enjoyed getting to know you

That I would love to take you to Kew
To spoil you for the day
And have a walk,
A talk,
Tea and cake
What do you say?
And then lastly to the gift-shop
To give you a keepsake

Love you Angie
And thank you
For being my guardian angel
And my favourite blue minion

Dazzling Donna

You are a mere 53
And yet you fail to see all that I can see
In you I mean
With you I hope I make you feel seen
You really don't look a day over forty
And I love that you are sporty

You have a really beautiful soul
And when you're around you make me feel
whole
As you have such a fire inside
That I love being by your side

I wish you were all mine
As you are so gorgeous and so fine!
I love you from your head to your toes
And I hate that you experience lows
Just know that I would be there to support you
As I understand the despair and the hopelessness
too
And I would never leave you on hold
As you are more precious than platinum or gold

I miss you when you are not here
As I have grown rather fond of you my dear

And God you have such a special heart
That it makes me sad when we have to part
Because you are so much fun
And time spent with you leaves me warm like
the sun

God I really am a lost little EllieWelly
Sitting alone just watching the telly
I get so sad when it's time to say goodbye
As it often feels like we've just said Hi

I enjoy it when we go for our little park stroll
And it was funny when you nearly fell from a
doggy-made hole
I just want to spend more time with you
And I hope that you like my company too

You showed me pictures of your dog Dingle
And I love when you walk because you jangle
and jingle
And you have such squeaky trainers too, which
would made us both laugh
And I love your tattoos that spiral from your foot
to your calf

You shine so bright
And when you go it's such a sad sight
Because you really are one precious star
That I get to see up close and not just from a far

God I really do love you loads
And with you I feel safe down all the backroads
Miss you more than you could know
Because you bring out the best in me and my
inner glow

Warrior Queen

You are a beautiful diamond of a race
With stunning dark features and ethereal grace
You have such a beautiful face
And I love your fast pace
Especially the way you stride
With your childbearing hips that are wide

I adore your lilac Crocs
And I love how you wear little ankle socks
But are you a woman who takes her whisky on
the rocks?
Or are you more like a sex on the beach?
Just simmering there out of my reach

You are such a stunner
But I feel you are a lady of leisure rather than
that of a track and field runner
Or did I get that wrong?
Because boy girl you are strong!
And that is something I admire in you
As you are helping me see this hospital
admission through

You are a Sunday school girl

That I would love to take on the dance floor for
a whirl

And you wear the blue well
And you are rather swell
Well in my eyes anyway
So who cares what the rest have to say

Love you diva
You little minx!

With you by my side
I don't feel the need to hide
But can actually share and confide
On this road of recovery
Or moreover a new found discovery
Of myself
And my mental health

Thank you Kosi for everything
You have helped lessen the sting
And helped me relearn how to sing

Love you forever
My sparkling diamond

Goodbye And Thank You

There's nothing like a goodbye
Yet its weird
As it feels like we've just met
And said hi
And introduced ourselves
As Megan the Ward Psychologist
And Ellie the patient
In desperate need
Of an understanding ear
And a calm guidance
Or moreover some direction
And some serious intervention
If not a resurrection
But you have pulled me through
Back to the present
Or more or less

There's so much to thank you for
And all the work we have done will remain
In place
And in my memory
You are now a chapter in my life
One piece of my ever growing puzzle
And a part of the ongoing support
That I need

And will always need
A part of my recovery
Which will be a journey
One with many a discovery
About myself
But also how I see others too

I have already learnt so much from you
And have found your style of therapy
comforting
And easy to follow
Your friendly manner
Has enabled me to open up
And engage fully
With each session
That I am sad to say goodbye
As I feel there is so much still to do
And learn
And all I want is to continue on with you
But sadly all good things come to an end
But you are sending me off in a better place
With more tools
At my disposal
And the knowledge that I won't be forgotten
And I'm not just another patient
Which is nice
As you're not just a psychologist to me
You're Megan the kind hearted psychologist

The one who has inspired me to write so many
rhymes
About all our times
Spent together
Talking
And laughing
As we unlock
And unpick
My fruitloop mind

God you've been great
But I really do hate
That this is goodbye
And my heart does let out a cry
And a deep and solum sigh
As I really
And I mean really
Don't want to say goodbye
To you
One of the most wonderful human beings to
walk this earth
God I feel so honoured
Grateful
Blessed
And forever thankful
To have worked with you Megan
And I can't thank you enough
For your time
Effort

Reassurance
And checking in
It's been short but sweet
And an absolute treat
Getting to know you Megan
So thank you for always being
So open
Honest
And you guessed it…
Setting boundaries
And teaching me about boundaries
I still need some work on those but I'll get there
So thank you Megan
For everything

My Inspiration, My Muse

Oh my dear Fiona
You are my Mona
My Mona Lisa
With such a warm smile
And a golden heart too
That I am going to be sad
When I have to leave you
And your poetry oasis
Because it's been so great
Excellent in fact!
Especially because you are so down to earth
And you are so respectful of our views
All our views!
Like you have the patience of a saint
That I really don't know how you do it
I would lose my shit
Excuse my French!
And I would have them all sit on the naughty
bench
Yet you hold yourself with such poise
Such grace
And we race
With a pace
Through each poem
But it feels just right

And God you're a wondrous sight
On a Wednesday afternoon
That I'm glad it comes around so soon
As I look forward to when we speak
Because you really do make my week
And it's all because of you
And what you bring
This vivacious energy
A heartiness
And an easygoing warmth

You are so wise beyond your years
And you are my little oldie
My Beetles fan
And oh I can see you
With a beer can
You're so hip
That you hop
And you make my heart stop
And drop
At times
At the poems you choose
But with you
It's only I
That will lose
If I don't stick around
And I'm glad I do
As you come up trumps
Every time

Like you deliver
And have flow
Like a river
Even with interruptions
You soldier on
And nothing phases you

You're also down with the kids
Just FYI
Not an oldie
Far from it
You're a spring chick
With hair that can flick
And you understand my hell
Which makes it easy to connect with you
Because you really do know
And you're a fighter
And you've come through
Pulled your way
Out of the darkness
And you are here to stay
Which makes my day

With you I have a direction
And I feel a deep connection
Because I don't feel so lost
As you are my lightening
Helping me to see
And setting me free

To be the thunder
In whatever you take that to be
But you still fill me with wonder
And oh how I wish I could have your number
As you are a fab peer support worker
One of the best
With a treasure chest
Of creativity
And knowledge
Up your sleeve
That I don't ever want you to leave
You are a special spirit
And have your own survival kit
Which I could learn a lot from
And you have taught me so much already
That my poetry is starting to feel steady
Because of all your encouragement
And guidance
And you inspire me constantly
I may add
And oh I'm so glad
To have made your acquaintance
As you really are a supernova
Just remember you are the lightening
And sometimes it just takes a while for the
thunder to catch up
You are of course so much more than lightning
waiting for the thunder
You're Fiona

And you're amazing
So please don't you forget it!

You Don't Understand

You don't understand
That I can easily spend 10 grand
Without batting and eyelid
And oh how my mental health slid
Down
So far down
That I ended up at Rosebank
Or moreover
Hell on earth
A place where I was in pain
Driven insane
To whose gain
But you don't understand

I wish you understood
That there is so much more to me
Than my Bipolar label
But you can't see
That all I want is to be free
To live and love my life
Amongst all the strife
And not commit suicide
But sometimes all I want to do is hide
From you all the pain I'm in
And I don't care that I have kin

Because at times I just want to die
And that's me being honest with you
I could lie
But I can't be asked
I'd rather be honest
As honesty is the best policy
Well in my books anyway
But you don't understand

You don't understand
And you haven't a clue
About me
As I'm complex
And at times I can perplex
You
When I'm speaking in rhymes
And I put you and everyone under my spell
Or more like showing you my internal hell
Because I can
And I'm sorry
As it's disturbing
I've just been mistreated
Trapped in the back of a hospital van
Like a caged animal
Why do you think I acted how I did?
Like is it so strange
My behaviour
All I needed was kindness
And a saviour

Yet I got nothing
But you don't understand

I wish you understood
How you made me feel
As I struggled to know what was real
And yes I did steal
And I never knew what was the deal
Like things kept changing
The bar kept rising
And the post kept moving
Yet there wasn't even a goal post
And I would constantly be put up for the roast
A roasting of my life
When I put a foot wrong
And yes I am strong
But you mishandled me
And put me in positions that hurt
Injected the hell out of me
Like I still have a bloody lump in my butt!
And I would constantly cut
My arms to ribbons
Like I messed up my tattoo
And that's because I didn't know what else to do
As I just couldn't get through
To any of you
But you don't understand

You don't understand

Like I really wished you did
But you don't
And you never will
And that's why I will just take another pill
And will fall
Fall from the highest window sill
I don't want to kill
But I have so much rage
Too much for someone my age
It just bursts from me
And it only escapes when I am in hospital
Now what does they say
I wonder…
It has me questioning
Should I be in hospital?
It clearly does me no good
Especially from where I'm stood
But you don't understand

I wish you understood
I really wish you did
But you don't
I feel like an outcast
No one understands me
And my past
Like all I want to do is have a blast
That will just last
Forever
And ever

But that's just me having my head in the clouds
And oh how I wish I could make my dad proud
Like sometimes I see him in the crowd
But it's not him
Its just me imagining things
My mind playing tricks
I'm deluded
He's dead
He's moved on
To a better place
A place without pain
A place where he is safe
Looked after
Loved
Really loved
Oh I miss you so
And it makes me very low
At times
And that's why I have so many rhymes
Talking about you
Your life
And how much I miss you
My little heart breaks
The floor shakes
It quakes
With the amount of sadness that I feel
It's a wave
Or more like a tsunami
I just want to sit by your tree

To be close to you
Oh I wish you had seen your life through
But you couldn't stay
And that's okay
For you suicide was the only way
And I know you struggled each and every day
And so do I
And that's why I want to be in the heavenly sky
To be able to fly high
And to be free
But you don't understand

The Extended Money Commandments*

1. Oh money, how I wish you were free.

2. But it's not, and it doesn't grow on a tree!

3. It would be wise to stop chasing after treasure.

4. As you will end up maxing out for the pleasure.

5. And it would be good to learn; how to manage your finances, as this is an essential skill.

6. Like being able to organise your paperwork, so you can find your last bill.

7. And oh how I wish I had been taught more, on the complexities of money.

8. As when I was younger, I would drain my bank account, faster than a Duracell Bunny!

9. Which would result me dipping into the dreaded overdraft, to tied me over till payday.

10. And my uncle would retort : "You have this extraordinary ability, of finding ways to throw all your money away!"

*11. Which makes me question my sanity, why I toil so hard to store all my stash.

*12. Which I will just have to leave behind. So my question is: "What is the price am I willing to pay, to keep up with the Joneses and their never ending flow of cash?"

Blood Test

Arm resting,
pillow underneath.

Skin prepared,
antiseptic wipe.

Tourniquet tight,
vein found.

Sharp scratch,
skin breached.

Tight fist,
tube slotted.

Drip…
Drop.

Slowly. . .
Steadily…

Tube fills,
fist relaxes.

Tourniquet off,

tube removed.

Needle out,
small wound.

Cotton wool,
apply pressure.

Plaster on,
all done.

Coming back,
results in.

Repeat again,
blood test.

Miss Cheerful

Oh Dani boy
You always spread joy
Wherever you go
And you are far from slow
When you are on the ward
And you help us patients from getting bored
By taking time out
And playing games with us
And you even taught me your sudoku way
Which made my day
I must say!

You take things in your stride
And you are a person that I can confide
Because you listen to me
And help me to see
Even when I feel low
You help me to get back on the go

You are the medication Queen
And you are always to be seen
Especially when you wear the medication apron
Which is such a sight
Because it is so garish and bright!

You keep yourself calm and cool
That I'm sure we would've been friends in
school
And you truly are one of a kind
With such a quick and intelligent mind
And I really do have a lot of time for you
As you have helped me see things through

You have such a kind heart
And you have been with me from the start
Like your hugs are so warm and tight
And you are such a wondrous sight
Because you always help me out
Even when I get frustrated and start to shout

I have been at Primrose for quite a while
And what I'll miss is your laugh and smile
So thank you Dani
And keep doing what you do
Because there is no-one as good as you

Fabulous Fola

45

You are a true beauty Queen
Who is forever seen

And you are simply divine
And you can shut me down with one line
But your words are sweet and sublime
And oh how you smell like cut thyme

God you are so lovely to me
So precious
So wonderful
So angelic
For all to see

You are my one and only
And without you in my life I am so very lonely
Because you really are special
And I hope you can feel the love
Because you are heavenly like a dove

When you're around
Your feet barely touch the ground
Or make a sound
Like you're so quick
So slick

At your job
And I am little Bob
Your yellow blue minion
Following you around in adoration
And you can always tell when I am blue
But you can always get through
To me
And make me see

Like you are so on the ball
And you were there when I had my fall
But you patched me up
Like a little pup
And you looked after me like a little child
Even though I was so very wild

You are a mother of four
And you have a pure heart to the core
That I hate when you leave out the door
As it makes me want to cry on the carpet floor
Because you are my mama bear
And oh how you care
About little old me

I love you with all my heart
And I never want you to depart
From me
Ever!
Because you really are one of a kind

A true diamond so rare to find

You are a real blessing
To me
And everyone you meet
And I love just taking a seat
By your side
Where I can confide

But it's time for me to say goodbye
And move on
As I'm in a better place
But I really will miss your lovely face
And how you hold yourself with such grace

My Greek Goddess

You are so cool, calm and collected
And you are very well respected

Because you have such flare
And I love your candy floss hair

You are so fine
Like that of French matured wine

And like me you love to cook
And when you got hurt it left me shook

Because you are so lovely and kind
And you are a person who just speaks her mind

And there is nearly always a smile on your face
And you walk at such a fast pace

That I really do like when we get to go for a
walk
Because we can just talk and talk

And time spent with you just goes by
Especially when gazing up at the blue sky

I really will miss your face
When I have gone from this place

Because you have seen this hospital admission
through
And you have been there for me when I've felt
blue

You get your patients notes done
And you always make time so we have some fun

You really have a beautiful soul
With such dark eyes like coal

And you have a real heart of gold
And when winter comes you really do feel the
cold

But on the ward you help calm things down
And your face rarely wears a frown

That I will really miss you Vasiliki
As you have helped me to see
All that I can be

So keep shining like a star
Because that is what you are.

My Bubble

It's my world
My universe
And my private sanctum
Of inner thoughts
Feelings
And emotions
Tripping over one another
Trying to be seen
To be heard
And to be acknowledged
But no
They are pushed to the furthest parts of my brain
And left alone
Taking up space
And waiting to be unearthed
To be recognised
And to be heard

But time passes
And years go by
More like decades
And the feelings
And thoughts
Are still there
But they're now are a distant memory

Of a time long ago

And my bubble remains
Intact
And still the same
Like a comforting blanket
Or more like a tight hug
It's welcome embrace
Never ceases to amaze me
And I feel safe
And can rest easy
Knowing I have you
My friend
And my companion
By my side

There's so much we have been through
Like the Rocky Mountains of my childhood
And the waves of sadness
Misery
And grief
That followed me around
It was this inner turmoil
That I could not shake
And left my inner world broken
That my bubble was needed
And I came to rely on it
As it was my safety net
And it kept me grounded

But also I was lost inside it
Not knowing what I felt
Just this numb pang
This sense of freedom
That I was lacking
Too scared to step out from its warmth
Or moreover it's shadow
Not knowing what to do
Without its guidance
Its help
And it's ever presence
In my life
Still
My bubble remains

Monday's At Two

I am so blessed to have you
And I look forward to Monday's at two
Because I get to spend a whole hour with you
Where I am able to just talk things through

You have helped me to acknowledge
And see
All that I can be
From my inner strengths
To my attributes too

We have spent time exploring
My bubble
And my inner world
Of thoughts
Emotions
And feelings

And I am slowly learning
But my heart is still yearning
To fix the hole
That's inside my soul

You have taught me so much
That I no longer need you as a crutch

Because I am starting to feel better
Within myself
And my overall health

And with you by my side
I don't feel the need to hide
But can be my authentic self
And I now have the tools to look after my
mental health

I have come a long way
And I really have been listening to what you
have to say
As you have help keep the daemons at bay
And I really did miss you in May!

There is something so special about you
And your approach in getting through
To me
And the chaos I have inside
Which I often try to hide

I am so lucky that I have you Helen
Because you are so easy to talk to
That I look forward to each week
Because I am able to speak
At length
Of what is on my mind
And there is a lot to unpick and find

The world really is a better place
Because you're in it
With your warm
And welcoming smile
And your infectious laugh too
That it's hard to stay blue
When I am around you

I have been in your safe hands
For quite a while
With your gentle guidance
And listening ear
That I am going to miss our Monday's at two
Because I have really enjoyed working with you
And getting to know you too
So thank you Helen
For all that you do

In The Kitchen

God I love to cook
But I often go off book
When following a recipe
As I struggle to stick to it
But that's just me
And my style
And I do take a while
At choosing what to make
Especially when baking a cake

There's often a lot to do
Even when making a simple stew
And it's best to get everything ready
So that things can run smooth and steady

Like cooking really does take skill
And you can often rack up quite a bill
When buying fresh ingredients
And kitchen equipment too
But it's all worth it
As it will aid you
In all that you do

There is so much fun to be had
Even when things go bad

But some people just get mad
Which is sad
Because mistakes are how you learn
Like when you get your first burn

And baking is a true science
Or moreover a real art
Because not everything goes together
And it takes time
Like writing a rhyme
And it's not a race
So just go at your own pace

There is so much to learn
And take in
That it can leave your head in a spin
As cooking demands a lot
Because you're learning on the spot
And often spending hours by a pot

But you will start to find
That cooking will take over your mind
And capture a piece of your heart
And also play a big part
In how you view food
Because the healthy stuff will lift your mood
And it will change the way you lead your life
Like the way in which you now use your knife

www.ingramcontent.com/pod-product-compliance
Lightning Source LLC
LaVergne TN
LVHW021239200726
843509LV00012B/1535